Introduction

These ideas aren't the only views possible of existence. They are wonderful if you can relate to them. If not, they are wonderful.

Question and Answer: Part I

Q: Do you describe the human race being as perfect as it is? As perfect as any other manifestations of nature? You also said that we don't have to be responsible for what we do or who we are. This is quite different from Buddhist teachings that encourage self-restraint and self-knowledge.

DB: At first glance, it seems so. Many spiritual teachings students believe that these teachings aim to improve their lives by putting in a lot of effort. Many practices are done in the hope that they will become an enlightened person.

It is assumed that an enlightened person is one who experiences no unpleasant emotions like anger, sadness, jealousy or fear.

These students want to get out of these problems and find a way to be happy and calm all the time. They are looking for a way to understand and master the negative aspects of life.

After many years of practicing self-development, they are now wondering why it hasn't worked for them, what they feel is wrong, and what they can do to improve their lives.

This is because the so-called "enlightenment" that these traditions offer has absolutely nothing to do self-improvement and control.

It's possible to practice monitoring your thoughts and emotions, analysing them, and trying to overcome them. But there is a fundamental delusion that doesn't get addressed. That delusion is what these teachings ultimately are about.

All great spiritual teachings point to freedom, which has nothing to do self-improvement and control.

Q: What freedom does that mean?

DB: Realizing that life is not our work; it's a natural movement. Everything is as it is at any given moment. There has never been anyone who can accomplish anything.

Q: Could you expand on this?

DB: Yes. Everything is changing if we look at life. Every moment is changing for even the most stable "thing" that exists.

It's easy to see this in things that are constantly changing, like thoughts, moods and emotions. But it's harder to see when things change slowly, like walls, furniture and mountains. If we really think about it, however, we can see that everything is constantly changing.

This house that we live in will eventually become dusty and dry if it isn't kept up. It is not likely that it will remain brand new for hundreds of decades and then age overnight. It is more like it is aging slowly, and it is changing in subtle ways.

It's easy to see that trees that have fallen into a forest are decomposing. They are slowly disappearing, becoming powdery, and eventually, those tiny bits of powder will seem to vanish. Actually, the form of a tree is a movement. It begins as a seed and grows into maturity before eventually disappearing.

It is the same for everything. The Himalayan Mountains are increasing one inch each year while other mountain ranges are reducing in height and becoming flatland. It was once home to an ocean, but that is no longer the case. The landscape around us is changing rapidly.

Hot gases formed the planet earth. They then became molten rock and then lava. This rock will change appearances until eventually it disappears. Astronomers can see entire galaxies disappearing from existence in faraway reaches of our universe.

We see constant movement in life. We can see the same thing happening in our bodies: breath coming and going; heart beating; thoughts flowing; moods shifting; perceptions changing; sounds dancing, twinges and pains, pulsations and vibrations.

Every moment of existence is a dynamic, moving event.

It doesn't really matter what it might be -- an atom or thought, sound, situation, body, mental state, plant, storm, mountain, or galaxy. Everything we know is constantly changing. There is only one constant: change and flux, inward and outer, large and small. This may allow you to see that all that really exists is this shift and flux.

There is no object or "thing" that can be truly created anywhere. Nothing is ever defined or established. Nothing is ever made to be, to remain, or to "be".

We often think of the universe as a collection of things. But, it's actually a great spirit. This is because it is vital and flowing.

It's sometimes called an unformed presence or simply "unform" in some spiritual traditions. Constant change refers to the continual absence of a particular arrangement or form.

This constant flow is not a fantasy situation. It is all that has ever been experienced. It is everything we are, and everything around us. There is no unformed life, inward or outward.

It is sometimes called energy, dark energy or quantum energy. Some refer to it simply as consciousness, Atman, God, Tao or Atman.

It is obvious that a presence or happening that changes constantly cannot be called anything specific. It is an ever-changing dynamic. This vital event is essential for a profound shift in our sense of life.

Existence can be seen as a collection. There is hope that one "thing" will never change. It is also possible to describe and understand existence. This perspective can lead to a lot of unhappy because it refuses to see the dance that is life.

Life should be something we can identify as something good, something secure, something that is pleasant and definable. Existence isn't something in particular. It is simply an ever-changing event without any intrinsic form.

The belief in form is constantly challenged by the movement of existence. That movement will always challenge any false impressions of stability and leave feelings of frustration, confusion, or sorrow.

It's possible to see that everything, even you, is in motion. There's no way to expect stability. It is just a magical dance that changes appearances constantly.

The body will not stop growing older if we ask it. It will not change if we ask it to. The body will eventually experience sickness, ageing and death, despite our best efforts.

Ask your circumstances to not change or only to go in positive directions. They won't. This is also true for all your thoughts, feelings and perceptions, as well as mental activities, states, and other apparent things.

Waves appear and disappear. The breath exhales and inhales. The heart relaxes and clenches. The alternating appearances of sound/silence and light/dark as well as hot/cold, joy/sorrows, clarity/confusion, and the pleasant/unpleasing are all possible.

Life is a constant flow of change, whether it's the changing of our moods, views, bodies, weather conditions, or the environment. This is happening and there are no controls.

It is possible to try to stop it by controlling thoughts, emotions and health. However, such efforts can only have limited and temporary effects. It doesn't matter how hard you try to make your life pleasant.

Life is a constant dance of ups, downs for everyone. This allows us to recognize that there will always be difficult periods. Sometimes, difficulties are extreme because this is how the natural rhythm of existence expresses itself.

This is one of the most important facts to know. This simple recognition of the obvious rhythm dissolves all confusion and useless struggle. Most of us feel like we are being subject to the cruel, cold whimsy of existence. We feel that we are being abused and separated from it. Let's take a closer look at it.

You may be surprised to discover that everything happens by itself, whether you are sitting or lying down.

Breathing happens without anyone being there. The heart beats the same way. The rods and cones in the eyes allow for seeing without the need to be touched. It is as easy as hearing, touching, tasting and smelling. Feelings, thoughts and moods are fleeting. The nervous system works; blood circulates; hair is grown; and so forth.

All this happens by accident. It's all just happenstance.

We didn't grow as a fertilized egg inside the womb. We didn't choose to start thinking, talking, thinking, or growing outside the womb. There is no "self" that directs this. It happens as a compulsive flow in nature.

Our bodies are not created by us, nor our brains. We are not the creators of our physical, mental, or lack thereof. We don't have the ability to create all of the needs, concerns, and interests that may arise at any given moment. All of this happens naturally.

It is impossible to choose to be someone else. Although it may seem like we make decisions, these decisions are made out of the needs and interests and concerns at any given moment. There is no "self" that makes them happen.

Nature presents situations that require a decision. The response is a movement by the only body, need and interest that nature also presents.

We do not have this body or this need, interest, or ability. We are this body and this need, interest and ability. If you just sit still and do not exert effort, you can see the movement you are expressing -- the dance of vibrations, thoughts and moods, pulsations and vibrations -- but you will never have the experience of any movement owning you.

Some people are drawn to art and some to science. Others gravitate to social service, family, business, religion, technology, etc. Science is not something you can choose to do if your primary love is art.

Every person's experience shows that everything we are and do is just the movement of existence. This is where we reach the greatest realization in all of the great spiritual traditions: We do not exist apart from the flow nature, and that flow is an unformed inexplicable dance that accomplishes itself.

Q: Are you saying that we don't have free will.

DB: I don't think so. Be very cautious with your descriptions of existence. They can cause a lot of fear and confusion. It's impossible to define everything if it is all acknowledged as it is, always-shifting and unformed. The only thing we have ever seen is unformed dance. It is the vibrant, pulsing and luminous moment that this moment is. It's all that.

Q: That can't be true. I mean that I have decided to ask these questions, and you have decided to answer them in the same way. It's your free will.

DB: Yes. But the decision you made was based on an interest in spiritual inquiry. It is a result of your apparent understanding and need to be spiritually informed.

It didn't happen that you decided at one point in your life to have this interest, understanding, or need. While you are here, someone else is surfing or studying international banking. You can't do anything about it. All you can do is be the person you are right now.

Spiritual inquiry is something I have a strong interest in. It's not something I created and cannot ignore. If you are serious about this subject, I will answer your questions.

I can't decide what my answer will be. I can only respond in one way. Nature presents me with that response. I cannot choose to be another person.

Q: For you, it's all automatic; everything happens automatically.

DB: Yes. It is possible to also speak spontaneously or organically.

The universe is composed of many things that all work together to create a single movement. They are also one movement.

All forms are in motion. All forms, or "thingness", are illusions. There is no way to see that they are not real.

A rope can appear to be a snake if not clearly seen, and a mirage may seem to water. The completely unformed, mysterious dance of this moment could also seem to be people in the world. However, this is a false appearance.

Q: You're claiming that this is enlightenment.

DB: This is what we call enlightenment. However, it's not the actualizing of a phenomenon that can be described in any way. This event cannot be described in any way, not even the description that a person becomes enlightened.

It's just the unformed, luminous and pulsing dance this moment is. Although it appears to be many things, these appearances are false. They are all unstable forms. There is constant movement and no explanation.

Q: It is pure knowing.

DB: That's not true.

Q: What's the point of knowing this?

DB: Nothing. "Knowing" can be a meaningless label.

Consider this: A newborn has no label for existence. There is no storyline, no "knower", "knowing" or "object of knowing". It's all the same basic warming and cooling, soundings, silencings, lightenings, darkenings, tingling, and trembling that this moment is. But there aren't any labels. It is a mysterious event.

If I point at something near, such as this, and ask you to explain it, you will give me a sound, the sound of "chair" but that sound isn't what I'm pointing towards.

When I ask a newborn what it is, they won't answer "chair". The child does not have any sound or symbol for anything. It's a mysterious, unlabeled happening. The so-called child doesn't have to answer any questions; it's just a meaningless "blah blah blah".

Labels will eventually arise, but sounds like "chair", "knowing" or "child" are no more meaningful than sounds like the "dizzlydonk and "wotafaroo".

Existence is a mysterious event. Its emergence is mysterious and it doesn't matter what labels or sounds are made, it will always remain a mystery. The barking of a trained seal does not explain existence. It doesn't matter how many barks we make, neither do we.

Q: How does this feel to be freedom?

DB: At any given moment there is an unformed, mysterious happening that moves on its own. However, there's the odd belief that it's a self -- living in, and "knowing" -- a universe of "things." However, it is a mysterious event. There's the delusion that it's being explained and then the delusion it has something wrong.

It's easy to get attached to the story of me who is directing and knowing life. I feel like it's not being done correctly because it's never how it should be. To feel better, there's a general sense of guilt about our perceived shortcomings and judgments of others as more flawed.

It's a constant struggle to fix ourselves and all other things. There is also a lot of frustration and sadness at the fact that nothing seems to be getting fixed.

All of this is a fantasy. It's a completely inexplicable phenomenon that exists. It is a completely inexplicable phenomenon. This realization brings a tremendous sense of relief, and rest.

Q: Is there anything wrong? We have wars, starvation and brutalities all over the globe. You can't say that there is anything wrong?

DB: These natural expressions of life are called the natural manifestations of existence. You'll see the same cruelty and hardship in any environment, whether it be forest or ocean. This is where the problem lies. We assume that we exist independently of the natural movement and are in control of it.

It is a lie to think we are in control of our existence. All that we are is an expression nature. Our efforts are not the only thing that holds existence together; nature's movements are what we make.

Our bodies, mental and physical abilities, as well as our needs, desires, understandings, and concerns are not our creations.

Q: It doesn't sound very liberating to find out that I am a complete slave.

DB: I don't think so. There is no one that can be separated from existence. It is not pushing you around. It's not you that you seem to be or do.

Your expression is the same as the stars of the night sky or any other appearances of nature. What could possibly go wrong with you? Which snowflake is making a mistake? What squirrel is making a bad decision in squirreling? Which storm is making bad decisions in its life?

Everything is possible to be at any given moment. This doesn't mean that everything is easy or flows in a pleasant manner. It acknowledges that life is what it is at any given moment and it is not personal.

Einstein stated that we are part of the movement and therefore no more responsible than an inanimate object (such as a stone) for our actions.

According to the Upanishads, "you" can be liberated when all is seen as a movement of God. The dance is all that you are apart from.

Buddha said, "What is not formed; descriptions don't apply." Realizing this ends any belief in stories about 'me' or 'mine', my existence, or my doing.

In the Bible, God, the great Spirit declares, "I am the I Am" (the fundamental happening, the areness, and the isness). I create light, darkness and peace; I do everything.

All cases have an indefinable presence or event that appears to be many things. However, those appearances are false. Stories of you and I, in various forms, about one thing influencing another are fantasies.

Q: However, if we believe that we are not responsible for our actions, it can lead to chaos. We could end up doing terrible things, or even give up altogether if we don't feel responsible.

DB: The mind may reject these ideas out of irrational fear when it first hears them. You have just listed some of the objections it raises. It may worry about becoming a mindless robot. Does that not mean we are robots if we obey the laws of nature? This raises fears about determinism or fatalism.

We may believe that we will be stuck in a fixed, mechanical way of being human. There is no hope for improvement. And we will eventually stop thinking about what's important.

This is the power and illusion of fear, the irrational fear that an ego will lose control. But, all the time, there has never been an ego in charge. Recognizing the vibrating flow of life doesn't mean you feel apathetic or ineffective. It gives rise to wonder and amazement at a magical presentation.

Understanding that we are the dance of the universe doesn't allow for disorder. It does not make us irresponsible. Even if a planet knew it was an expression of the universe it would not be able leave its orbit. The orbit is part and parcel of that expression. It is the same for us.

The feeling of responsibility you feel isn't something you create. It's an expression that nature has given you. Love is not your creation. It's an expression of nature. Thinking is not your creation. It wouldn't exist if it didn't exist.

Give up everything that is not important to you and everything that you hold dear. Give up all your needs, desires, and concerns. It's impossible because you are not able to exist apart from what is being presented.

Do nothing, but just do it. You'll eventually get something. You must eat, drink, get up, and go to the bathroom. This is the compulsory movement that defines you. Even the urge to rest and sit is a voluntary, obligatory action.

It doesn't matter if you are the boss of a large corporation or a nun contemplating in a cave. All of it is an inexplicable event.

Realizing that you don't do terrible things is not going to make you more likely to do them. Your personality is not yours. While some people do horrible things, many do not. It was not decided by the human race that it would be like this; it is simply how it is.

This is not a robotic existence. You are not being programmed or pushed around by anyone else. All that is available is the wild fullness and freedom of your existence. That fullness is all that exists.

This illusion of form is infinitely creative. There are no two forms of form ever identical. Every moment is unique. There have never been two identical things. No two snowflakes, no two leaves, no two trees, no two moments.

Because it is constantly changing and vibrant, it is unpredictable. It never repeats itself. Although some general predictions are possible, the details are often unexpected. You can even be completely wrong with predictions. Just look at the weather forecasts.

Q: Life is out of control.

DB: Control ideas don't apply here; there is only motion. This flow is characterized by an inherent order or current. It is sometimes called an innate intelligence. This is how a plant grows. The plant grows in this order, twisting and turning until it becomes recognizable, even though its appearance is not the same as any other.

The plant doesn't require control. It isn't conscious of its actions. It doesn't keep itself together by exerting effort, and it doesn't decide its direction. It is not a controllable process. It's not like it is for you?

Q: How did you get this sense?

DB: It just happens. You could have a life story that describes key moments of your life, but it would only be a fantasy. Existence has no form and explanation.

Q: You have thoughts and stories.

DB: Not exactly. The movement we call thoughts or stories is still occurring, but it's an indefinable event.

Infants don't understand anything. Existence is an inexplicable buzz or tingle. It is still. It doesn't really matter how many dance forms are there, or how many sounds appear and disappear, it all comes down to one unformed dance.

Q: This doesn't help me understand it.

DB: There is no understanding.

Q: Can you tell me more about the process of awakening?

DB: If you'd like me to, I will.

Q: What is the story behind this?

DB: It appeared to happen over a lifetime with specific realizations occurring in particular moments.

There were times when everything seemed like one big thing from an early age. In my twenties, it was difficult for me to understand how anyone could "make" decisions. These decisions are a result of interests and abilitles that no one creates.

A book that claimed no one had ever experienced directing life was something I came across years later. It was obvious that this statement was true when I reflected on it. Nature is the movement that causes us to have bodies, needs and interests.

There was initially fear and confusion surrounding all this because it seemed like "I" was losing command. But, it soon became clear that everything was happening by itself.

It became clear that existence cannot be defined. It doesn't make sense to identify forms, since existence isn't defined by form. Everything is constantly changing. Stories about form cannot be true. Stories about me growing up and reading books, and then coming to realizations, can't possibly be true.

It's easy to be fascinated by the appearance of existence. There is an attachment to its sounds and looks. But existence doesn't have a particular feel or look.

It is likely that whatever it appears to be right now will soon change. It is changing in every way: feelings, moods, thoughts, and sounds are changing.

It is an inexplicable, lively dance that has no form. It's impossible to stop, and nobody can stop it.

Q: What do you think about spiritual practices to awaken?

DB: The majority of so-called spiritual practices attempt to control and develop something. They are based on the belief that you can control your existence.

These practices cannot transcend the belief that they are in control. They are the belief that you can make something happen through practising.

This belief cannot be broken. It is possible to see what is actually happening and realize that there is an indefinable, dynamic event that is accomplishing its own goals. The basic nature of life is clear when you just sit down and do nothing. This is the deepest meditation in any spiritual tradition.

While some may consider it a practice of meditation, others argue it isn't. You're doing nothing. It's called satsang in Advaita, which means association with being.

It doesn't mean that we have to do nothing. But it is only when we are doing nothing that everything becomes apparent.

This is the underlying message of all great spiritual teachings, regardless of what they may offer. It doesn't matter if it's called meditation or satsang.

You're welcome to do nothing in any of these cases. Life may be the miraculous event it is.

It is possible for belief in form or personal doing to fade, and all that is visible is the vibrant, undefinable happening that everything really IS. Some traditions believe there is only God and Atman. However, these labels are not a description of the unfathomable life that exists. It doesn't matter what you call it, that's part and parcel of the dance.

It will take you thirty years to achieve this, and there are others that tell you it can be done immediately. However, they all share one thing in common. It doesn't matter if it appears to happen after thirty years of hard work, or if it happens while listening to someone talk about it or by chance. It's the realization of everything being unformed, indefinable and just presenting itself.

This realization will make all descriptions and stories fall apart. Threety years of work will be viewed as fantasy. All stages of development will be considered fantasy. Enlightenment will also be considered fantasy. These descriptions are false. It has never happened that anyone did anything or arrived anywhere. There is no moment.

The illusion that an ego is controlling its life is so common that almost everyone has a desire to control it. There is a common assumption in spiritual circles that teachings must focus on controlling something. It is common   to try to control or create perfect health, perfect peace, perfect love and perfect concentration. This misses the essence.

Q: *Which is?*

DB: Realization. Alan Watts used the expression, "It's false that you came into this universe; you emerged from it like a flower emerges from a plant." The whole universe is doing what you are doing.

Q: You've been meditation since you were fourteen years of age. You can be sure that this effort led to the understanding you now have.

DB: That statement is completely absurd. If you claim that one thing causes another, it is actually saying that there is only the motion of the universe. This is how the story of cause-and-effect ends.

This understanding was caused by meditation. Then, we need to ask, "What caused the meditation?" It could be attributed to my personality, ability, or need. What caused these things? It could be that my genetic makeup and my upbringing were both factors.

What was the root cause of these things? Then, we need to think about my parents, their genes, their upbringing, my grandparents, great-grandparents, and so forth -- all the way back through human history.

But, all that happens in the cosmos supports humankind, so we need to also look at the causal chain. The planet is home to human beings because of the availability of oxygen, water, heat, and light. These conditions are created by the movement of the galaxies, and the galaxy exists because it arranges itself in the way it does.

Recognizing the whole movement of cause-effect allows us to see the whole of the universe. After that, there are no more causes because it is impossible to find anything else.

If you truly believe in the chain effect of cause and effects, then you cannot believe that there is a separate being accomplishing any task. Every atom in your body -- every thought, word, and deed you make -- is an expression the chain.

Q: I was trying to point out that spiritual practices can help people become enlightened.

DB: Yes. It appears so. But, this is obviously not the case. Only a small percentage of those who have awakened from the practice over the centuries of hundreds of thousands of them are believed to have done them.

This is not to mention the fact that spiritual practices can also be a source of awakening for people who do not practice them. Einstein was an excellent example, Spinoza another. They simply acknowledged their scientific observations.

One man was just walking cattle back from the barn, when he realized that everything is the movement and nature of nature. Another was involved in brothel sex. Another was sick and spitting blood when this realization occurred spontaneously.

One day, a young Japanese girl was dying. She realized that all things are connected. In India, a boy stopped believing he was a person and began to accept the inexplicable events of existence.

According to Buddhist scriptures, many people were able to wake up after listening only to the Buddha's talks. Advaita traditions include similar stories about other teachers.

Although this so-called enlightenment can be found in nearly every situation, there is no one approach, no method or technique that guarantees it will happen.

I am not suggesting you should not practice spiritual practices. You don't need to worry about that because everything is a movement in nature. This includes your life and any so-called awakening.

Only nature can give us the body, needs, interests, urges, and actions that we need at any given moment.

Q: Is there any way to be enlightened?

DB: In reality, there is no way to be enlightened. The so-called awakening refers to the realization that nothing can be defined. Even the claim of someone becoming enlightened is not true. Focusing on stories about enlightenment is missing the wonder of life's full events.

We are amazed at the variety and texture of nature when we enter a forest. Every aspect of it is a marvellous expression of the universe -- every tree, leaf, blade of grass and bird. It is all a good thing.

We don't tell the gnarled trees that they should look like the tall straight trees. We don't tell them they aren't trying hard enough or not practicing enough. We don't tell our clients that they have gone the wrong way or should do something different. This would be absurd.

There is instead an appreciation for nature's beauty, wonder, and delight. It's a feeling that every apparent thing is part of the greater event called existence.

Go to the supermarket, and you will be amazed at how many people are waiting in line to pay their bills. Are we able to marvel at nature's amazing creations or are we prone to ranting about it? "Look at him acting like that -- what a fool! Look at her! She shouldn't dress like that -- she is too old!

At home, we do the exact same thing, staring at the mirror in the bathroom and thinking, "What's the problem with me?" This is unacceptable. "I should be something else or more." Perhaps we wish that we could all be enlightened and everything would be better.

The great spiritual traditions don't refer to an enlightenment as a way to live a better life. It's the realization of everything being exactly what it is at any given moment. It is all the complete, pure expression of the cosmos.

Q: Enlightenment cannot save the world.

DB: What can you save it from? Everything that appears is moving towards its essence. Every aspect of existence does it right, no more than any raindrop. It doesn't have to be unpleasant.

Existence is doing fine. In fact, it's doing everything for us. This realization dissolves our self-righteous arrogance. Nobody can take responsibility or hold someone accountable for their behavior. One cannot give credit or take blame for another.

Everything must function the way it does. It is your body, desire, interest, urge, or action. Whatever it appears to you now, it is already moving on to another expression.

It is a dream to believe that you can make it happen by your own efforts. Nature gives rise to all abilities, interests, actions. There is no need for personal effort. It's like assuming that a person deserves credit or blame for how they look and behave.

It is impossible to make mistakes in your life. Because whatever you think, say and do, it is just the inexplicable dance that is existence.

Q: However, we must consider the whole of life before taking any decisions.

DB: Logical thinkers believe so. Intuitives do not.

Q: *Your point is?*

DB: There are no two expressions ever the same. We cannot copy someone else.

According to the old story about children, a swan who tries to be a duck will feel out of place and ugly. A duck will also have difficulties trying to be a Swan.

Spiritual teachings help us to appreciate the amazing, unique and wonderful expressions of ourselves. We are not trying to turn ducks into swans. Ducks are fine. You can't go wrong with any animal.

Q: What should I do if a poisonous serpent tries to bite you? It's the natural expression and it's okay.

DB: I didn't say that. DB: Although there is nothing wrong with their expressions, certain snakes and certain people are naturally dangerous and we automatically respond to danger.

Nature automatically expresses all circumstances and all responses to them; it's one movement. Even if you try suppressing your natural reactions, they will eventually break through because we are nothing apart from that.

Q: Okay, but I still have questions about how to live my life after all this.

DB: While most people want someone to show them how to live, no one can tell you what to do or be. Each person is unique.

Spiritual teachers are sought by people who want to control their lives and make them happy. People ask many questions but the most important question is "How can I gain enough understanding and control to ensure that I don't feel lost, scared, sad, or uncomfortable?"

This is the answer: "You can't."

These great spiritual teachings are not able to provide an escape from the life's expressions. These teachings offer the possibility to dispel certain confusions but not by controlling them. It's through acknowledging certain facts such as the changing nature of all things.

Realize the present moment and let go of unrealistic expectations. It is possible to let go of the mistaken belief that form and personal doing are real.

The natural quality of life is one that gives you a sense of well-being. You didn't need to be happy as a child to enjoy life. It was an amazing experience, even though it was difficult and sometimes unpleasant. The event was fully realized and the focus was not on control and form.

Spiritual teachings offer an opportunity to acknowledge the vast, unformed, and vibrant event of life, as well as its inherent sense magic and well-being.

Although you may seem to be able to access many teachings both Eastern and Western in appearance, your unique way of living will still be the best. You cannot match any one expression of nature exactly, just like every other expression.

It doesn't matter what you do next. It will always find the next priority, the next interest, need, or concern. It was apparent to me as a four-year-old. At ten it was different. As a teenager it was quite another. It's currently whatever it is and will automatically change to another expression.

It may sometimes seem unclear and uncertain at times, but this is the natural expression of existence.

There is no one you. It's just the body, desire, interest, or urge that's presenting at this moment. Nature is already moving towards something else. It was someone who needed lunch before lunch. After lunch it is something else. It's someone who needs sleep before bed; it's someone who needs to get up in the morning.

There may be a major issue, and responses are available. It may move around in different ways for a long time but eventually it will find a completely new expression. This is the only unformed dance.

Realizing this gives rise to a greater trust in our ability to move, a sense wonder at the miraculous appearance of everything and a richness in the whole and vital expression of the present moment. It's easy to relax because we don't have to be held together. All that we think, say and do in any given moment is automatically presented.

Jiddu Krishnamurti used the expression, "Perfection can be found in this movement." This is the one movement that we never seem to understand.

Q: Do you want to make this clear to everyone?

DB: Not at all. This will only be of interest to a small percentage of the population. Other opinions may differ. There is nothing anyone can do to change that.

Reflections I

This perspective isn't the only way to see existence. It's only for those who can relate to it.

People coming together around a particular perspective have no greater significance or meaning than robins gathering alongside robins or crows gathering with crows. It's like clouds gathering in the sky. It's the inexplicable act of existence doing what it does.

Most people find it difficult to believe that Hitler is an entirely natural expression of existence.

While we accept that tigers and sharks don't usually attack humans, some do. Although they're not the norm of life, they're a hard fact of daily life. It is so hard to accept that other human beings can also express themselves in this manner.

Both saints and sinners can be valid expressions of existence. It is a misunderstood arrogance to condemn one over the next; they must both be what they are.

Both may seem gentle and passive while the other can be aggressive and nasty; they are different. Each is just an indefinable expression or existence, and they are equal.

If we were pushed around by the universe's movement, this would be a doctrine based on determinism. We are part of this movement, but we are not separated from it.

This is what tradition means when it speaks of the unconditioned. Because life's mysterious event is inexplicable and formless, it is unconditioned. There is nothing else.

Our conditioned behaviour is often mistaken for the unexplicable wholeness that is free to express itself. This is what "reaching the Unconditioned" means.

Although the ideas presented here may seem odd, others have shared similar views, including Albert Einstein and Simone Weil, Spinoza, Emerson.

To make their lives more simple, people want to wake up. It is obvious that not everything needs to be transformed; everything is already flowing to its true nature at any given moment.

Anyone who tries to conform to a standard of behavior is doing so in pain. It is difficult to accept that there are no universal standards for human behavior. Nature constantly creates unique expressions that can never be matched.

To try to deny your uniqueness is to suffer. It doesn't matter where you are at the moment, it will eventually become something else.

Mental agonies are caused by the belief that we are separate from all movement, a "me", who owns and directs thoughts, feelings and urges.

This concept is the basis of the karmic chain personal responsibility. It carries the guilt or pride of accomplishment. Realizing that we are a part of the greater happening of existence frees us from personal responsibility.

For those who are curious, it is possible to see that we are a movement of existence, the same movement as the stars in night sky and the migration flights wild birds.

Although we now appear the way we do, we could also appear as a pinch or drop of moisture. We will eventually appear that way; we are a happening without any particular form.

Spiritual awakening is the discovery of what is actually there, the mystery surrounding it. It appears to be something or someone, always shifting and moving, but never being anything in particular.

Freedom is the indefinable vitality of being free from all strain and effort. It doesn't eliminate the difficulties and pains of life, but it does end the illusion that all of these are being understood or directed.

Because all appearances are constantly changing, the various forms that appear in our lives can't be true to reality. It doesn't matter how a cloud appears, whether it is shaped like a person, house, or mountain, we know it's a Cloud. The unformed cloud is the reality, and the appearance of form does not reflect reality.

This holds true for all things: people, objects, feelings, emotions, moods and thoughts. Everything is changing and flowing. They are the passing appearances a great, unformed and inexplicable event -- a giant cloud or an event -- you can call it what you will.

All appearances are influenced by the nature of the universe in the same way that a cloud's appearances change to match its nature. This unformed, inexplicable flow is often mistaken for a collection of objects and its impersonal dance as an accomplishment by humans.

Because spiritual awakening is not about building an ideal society, it's realizing that our actions are only part of the larger movement of existence. Everything is, in every apparent moment, the complete and pure expression that nature is.

All that we have done, all that we are doing now and all that we will do in the future is a movement within the cosmos. The cosmos is that mysterious, spontaneously manifesting itself.

This is the freedom that the great spiritual teachings are urging us to realize. It is not about the freedom to create a fantasy world in which we and the world are perfect.

It is a strange notion that nature and nurture are different. As if the movement of existence is divided into parts that have an influence on each other. Many people wonder how much of who we are is "natural" and how much has been affected by poor parenting and societal education.

It is often overlooked that bad parenting and the functioning of society are natural expressions of our existence. The abilities of parents, and their lack thereof, are as much an expressions of nature as any other; the same applies to every person and action in society.

Nature and nurture are not compatible. Every thing that appears to be in existence, including the waves, tides and currents of the ocean, is actually just one movement.

Life doesn't move in any one direction. It's always here and now. It isn't moving in any particular direction. Dreams of progress, direction, evolution are fantasies.

The passing appearances and evolution of form are stories of direction, progress, and evolution. But form is a illusion. Any identifiable form or "thing" that appears to exist now is constantly changing and will eventually disappear. It is not changing into anything else, it is just an inexplicable form.

Ask three of your friends to join you at the table. Place a cup on each side of the table. Place the cup closest to your face and place the glass on the opposite side.

Tell your friends, now, that you are going to tell the truth about what's going on at the table. "The cup is infront of the glass."

"Wrong," replies the friend in front of you. "The cup is in front of it."

"Wrong," says the friend to your left. "The cup is to one side of the glass," the friend to your right says. "The cup is to your right."

All of this is wrong. You're wrong. Life is multi-faceted and cannot be described.

This is compounded by the fact that everything is constantly changing and there is no way to describe it. All things are fundamentally unformed. Even the feeling of existence disappears each night and reappears every day.

Descriptions of form can be misleading. It is impossible to explain the happening of existence in a true way. This realization is not another thought. It's the fading away of attachment to thought, which is the end of belief in description.

Existence manifests in unique ways every moment, despite its illusions of form. There are no identical items: there are no snowflakes, trees, leaves or beings.

There is no one way to be the same. One person may be concerned about the possibility of death when climbing Mount Everest. Another person might find it thrilling and challenging.

You can't manifest my manifestation. You can manifest however life presents you. You can't go anywhere else than where you are now.

Your manifestation is my honor and encouragement. It is impossible to know what it really is, and it is impossible for anyone to tell you what it should look like.

It is like saying that one person is doing something right while another is wrong. It makes no sense.

Taoist Echoes

All things are unified when they are viewed from the fundamental fact of change. It is an un-form presence. It is part of all appearances. They are expressions of its energy and nature.

Recognizing the unformed nature and inequalities of all things is the only way to relieve suffering.

Happiness and sadness are both temporary. It is impossible to hold on to one or the other. You are now brave, fearful, and now confused.

It's hard to change the way you live your life. It is not possible to consciously digest the food that you eat, or make your breath rise and pass. You can't control your blood flow, your interests or your understandings. Events happen naturally.

Reflections II

Because we are only capable of responding in one way to every situation, and with any response that nature may present, our instinctual   responses automatically work. All that matters is what pushes itself forward in any given instant.

However, this realization is not what most spiritual practitioners want. They desire a story about enlightened beings and a world that is moving towards a golden age. Instead of awakening from the dream world and self, they want a unique self and a different world.

It doesn't take much to allow life to flow. You can't exist apart from this.

It appears that matter can become energy; it appears that energy becomes matter; liquid appears as gas; it appears like gas has become liquid; heat appears become coolness; it appears like heat appears to be becoming coolness; and so forth.

It is not possible for matter to become energy. These are only the superficial appearances of a pulsing and surging un-form.

It looks like an cloud. In one moment, it appears like a person, while in another it appears like a house. The cloud is simply a change in appearance. It never becomes anything other than a cloud. Every aspect of existence is the same movement. It appears to be different things but it never becomes anything other than a happening.

While what is there is what is there, what appears to be it is not. It is constantly changing. This applies to all you appear to be, as well as all you think, say and do.

This isn't about attaching to another view; it's about acknowledging the vitality of a formless dance. This shifts the focus from the narrowness of thinking to the greater moment: the mysterious, sounding and darkening, warming, cool, cooling, pulsing and trembling event.

This is the moment that all sense of understanding or directing this happens disappears. This is not a state of mind we create, it's just the acknowledgment of what is.

It is impossible to imagine anything other than this event. The word

"I" is just a pointer. It's not the same as "over there". No matter if we look inwardly, "I", and outwardly, "over there", what we find is a vital, pulsing energy. This realization means that the word "I", while it may refer to an inanimate, formless event, does not refer to someone with a past.

Life can present itself in a variety of ways: confusion and clarity; anxiety and confidence; sadness and happiness; horror and beauty. These illusions of form change; they are born, they age and eventually die. But the unformed

life that is actually there, which is always present and always unformed, is never lost. It is all that is.

You don't need to train yourself to follow the flow. Everything we see and say and do -- all the beautiful stuff as well as all the mundane, boring, unattractive and unhealthy stuff -- is already part of the divine, mysterious flow. This is all there is.

It may seem unfair to some that certain people have relatively easy lives and others find themselves in very difficult situations. But, the fact that existence exists is not fair or unfair. It's a wonderful, mysterious, and sometimes painful dance.

Spiritual disciplines do not aim to balance or perfect the cosmos. In every moment, the wholeness of existence is already balanced.

It is easy to see that all existence is in flux. All things in the outside world are changing and we can see the same shift in our own inner world. It's not formed in here, it's unformed out there. It's not in here or there. It's just one event.

In Hindu tradition, the phrase "I am That" is used to signify the undivided nature all things. The literal meaning of the word universe is "undivided turning".

We can observe galaxies disappearing from existence in faraway regions of the universe as astronomers or as meditators, but all we have ever seen is unformed life.

All things move. It is foolish to call some of it birth or death. All that exists is an absence of form. How many times have you heard people say that everything changes? This belief is not a strange one. It's part of every person's experience with existence.

By focusing on the illusion of form that everything is, we lose sight of the lively, formless dance of all things.

Existence is not about me, an us or a world. It is an unformed, undefinable event that simply happens.

True compassion is impossible if "we" believe that they are independent from and in control of the events. Instead, there's arrogance about personal achievement or failure, and a sense superiority or inferiority.

Realizing that everything, including you, is an inexplicable movement that spontaneously expresses itself gives rise to wonder and amazement at all its manifestations.

It is a delusion to honor so-called individuals for what they have accomplished or denounce them for their mistakes. We are not made. Nobody directs their manifestation. No one is to blame or credit.

Preaching does not make morality the default. Each society has its own sense of what the tribe accepts and rejects. This is the same as language, which has evolved from the movement of nature.

We all agreed that there would never be language and that there would not be a moral sensibility. A refined sense of morality emerged as a result of the various cultures that we have.

Every culture and every person in it has their own sense of right and wrong. Nature manifests in many and different ways, yet again.

However, there are enough similarities to make it seem like there is one common morality. Most people view their own morality as the best and detest all others. This is another example of arrogance.

There is no common morality. Each person has a different sense of what is possible and what we can do. We all have our own opinions about what we can and can't do and how we can deal with it. These variations can be subtle or large. Human beings are not generally evil.

In extreme circumstances of war and deprivation, this can change. Different time periods have different moral standards. A person behaves differently at different times. Although fluctuations aren't usually large, they can be.

Reincarnation is a fantasy. Existence has never seen a repeatable form. The same thing that causes the shifting of galaxies to shift on the other side of the universe is the shifting of minds and bodies. This happens in any form. It is impossible for something to become another thing. There's only one great unformed event that will never be formed.

A bear-shaped cloud doesn't necessarily mean that it is a bear. You don't believe a cloud that looks like a horse is a bear. It's not true that there is a horse or a bear.

We aren't things becoming other things. You and I are an unformed phenomenon. This is not a place where form ideas are applicable. This realization is not about describing anything. This realization ends the focus on interpretations and thoughts. Instead, it's just a simple acknowledgment of the bigger, more mysterious moment that is.

The present moment is without form. This is evidently the nature of existence.

It is easy to recognize that planets move in the same way as the universe. Changes in landmasses, weather, plants, animals, and bodies are all part of the natural cycle.

Heart beats. Breath comes in and out. Blood circulates. Immune systems operate. It is as easy as seeing, hearing, touching and tasting. This happens without any effort.

It happens. Moods can shift, ideas can alter, perceptions can change. This event is us -- we don't exist apart from it -- but somehow we believe that we're doing it.

All religions point to an indefinable existence that is the foundation of all existence. It could be the unfathomable God in the Bible, the mysterious asankhata of Buddhist scriptures or the mysterious, unformed ocean in the Ashtavakra Gita. The story is the same.

Albert Einstein and David Bohm, scientists, claim that everything in existence is an indefinable phenomenon.

Both science and religion point to the same simple fact: All of existence is a vital presence which cannot be explained in any way. This includes you.

True humility is the realization of this event or its presence. This realization dismantles the illusions of independent will and arrogance about credit or blame. In realizing that we are all one of many appearances of nature, judgment is replaced with wonder and amazement.

Sitting still and not trying to make a difference in our lives will allow us to see the beauty of life. It just happens. There is nothing more to do. The truth is simple. The heart beats, the breath goes and comes. The heart beats; the pulse, pulsations and twinges of emotions, thoughts and feelings rise and fall. The urges rise and fall; some become actions while others don't; life flows.

There are many alternating appearances of this flow: clarity and confusion, joy, sorrow, hope, despair, and so forth.

Even though we try to avoid moving, we are compelled at some point to do so. We eat when we are hungry and rest when we are tired. We   are automatically able to function because of the movement and vibrations of certain pulsations. This is a natural process.

Artists, athletes, intellectuals and parents don't choose their dreams and hopes.

There is no peace until you realize that we are an indefinable activity. All things, all acts ions, all thoughts and words are passing manifestations of an indefinable, unformed event.

Who's behavior can go in any direction? Every person must live in accordance with the natural physical and mental capabilities that are available to them, focusing on the needs, interests and concerns that may mysteriously arise at any given moment. We are not anything else.

This realization imposes an unshakeable humility. It's not the self-absorbed virtues of cultivated virtues. Instead, it's the recognition that we cannot take credit or blame. Nobody can.

We cannot judge others' behaviour. Our apparent doing and their apparent doing are a movement of nature according to its physical makeup. It is impossible to do anything else.

This is what the average person fears. They imagine that this way of seeing will lead to some kind of disaster. Maybe we will stop trying and society will collapse. Maybe we will become completely irresponsible. It's possible that we'll become completely irresponsible if it isn't our fault.

This is an misunderstanding of the message. You cannot stop functioning in this situation. It's not about the realization that you are responsible for your non-functioning and functioning.

Your life is a reflection of the impersonal nature of nature. This event is the only thing that separates you from it.

This doesn't mean you can abandon the process or lose control. There is only one process. There is nothing else that is obvious; there has never been anything else.

A sense of responsibility and love are not something you can do on your own. All things are. Realizing this, you can respect all aspects of life: the horrors of some, the enchantment and wonder of others.

Knowing that we are not creating ourselves is a source of endless tolerance. It's a source of compassion to know that we all share this situation.

Life is more than a pleasant, relaxing experience. Mother Nature is generous in her expressions, but she also eats her young. This was reflected in symbols from the past -- mysterious, dark and powerful figures such as Shiva and Kali.

Today, it seems that we tend to see love and peace as the true essence of existence and all other things as defilements. This is not a good way to prepare for life. Life's dance is a natural expression of its emotions.

The perceiving system searches for patterns and formations within life's flow. The obsession with the illusion of form can lead to feelings of insecurity and separation. It is futile to hope for something stable to hold on to: a pleasure or understanding, a feeling, etc.

The search for stability is frustrating. There is no flow. It is unprovoked and unstoppable.

Life isn't going to do what we want. It doesn't have to be our fault. Life can move in any direction it wants at any given moment. We cannot stop it, both individually and collectively. This is the only way we exist.

Our bodies, our needs, interests, understandings and abilities are all part of the movement of nature. Each expression of nature is unique. It doesn't matter if it is unusually attractive from time to time.

While we can admire someone as much as we admire sunsets, we cannot use them to model us all.

What happiness could be found in rejecting any expression of nature but one?

Some teachers say that it is important to work towards morality, wisdom, as well as reducing personal greed. They are attracted to those who have a similar outlook. They find it so sad that others don't see what they see. However, it is a delusion for them to believe that everyone should care about their particular way of living.

Each expression is a result of the nature of existence. It sends different birds along their respective migration routes. Even if they appear to be on the same migration route, each expression is unique.

It doesn't matter what you feel compelled to do in your life, but it is absurd to assume that everyone should. Your way is not the only way. It's like ducks thinking that all birds should be ducks.

A goose flying south in winter is not concerned about why other birds aren't following him. He's also not judging other birds for not knowing their true migration route. He doesn't try and convince sparrows or robins to change their lives for his.

This so-called "enlightenment" is simply the recognition that all apparent things in existence are inexplicable events.

If you look outwardly, you can see an inexplicable event. But if you look inwardly, it's a mysterious happening. It's unformed here, unformed there; it's an unformed and undivided dance that does what it does.

This awakening is not always pleasant. It is replaced by absolute confusion as the impression of existence being understood and directed.

It is common for childhood views and adult views to be replaced by them. Some adult views may be replaced by extreme views, while others will lose their usual adult views. However, in a few cases, belief in any view is overthrown. As it becomes clear that every moment is an inexplicable, larger event, the focus of attention shifts away from thoughts and viewpoints.

This initial shift can be frightening and confusing. All descriptions are invalidated, and all senses of free will are eliminated. This shift can be seen to occur independently of what is desired. It happens regardless of whether it is wanted. It is not the result of individual effort. It's the result of the movement of existence itself.

Because it is the end of all hopes and dreams, this realization cannot be wished for. It is the end of a self that can't be described. Although this so- called awakening is not something you want, it might happen.

It's not a temporary mood or the loss of reality. This is the disappearance of fantasy. The only thing that remains is a mysterious, spontaneous dance that expresses itself as all things apparent, a magical parade passing by.

Although spiritual awakening is often described by the movement into silence or spiritual awakening, this description can be misleading. It is not the absence of physical silence that is being described. The vital, pulsing and sounding event that is actually happening becomes much more apparent than ever before.

The silence is the end to attachment to descriptions. The intellectually loud attachment to frantic thought and all its side effects is reduced or silenced and the bigger, more mysterious dance of the moment becomes apparent.

It doesn't need to be held in place because it lacks form. It is completely unintelligible, so there's no need to grasp it. It's all there is. Because each expression is unique, there's no need to force anyone to conform.

Fears of death are no longer rational. There is only the unfathomable dance in the cosmos. Blame and credit no longer make sense. Pride and shame disappear and it becomes difficult to judge others.

Obsessive thoughts, struggle, fear, shame, conformity and desire are all "silenced" in different ways. However, the vital, buzzing moment of the moment is not.

Existence manifests itself in changing appearances: light/darkness, sound/silence and warm/cold. Joy/sorrow, warmth/cold, clear/confusion, hope/regret and so forth. This is not a sign of failure; it is the essence of existence.

This is our reality. It moves to various expressions and displays different appearances when viewed as opposing. They're not opposed, they're just the multiple faces of the same dynamic.

It's not possible to wake up and feel this essential flow. But unnecessary confusions and struggles will disappear if you realize that this is your natural expression.

It can be frightening to realize that nature is free to express itself without regard for our desires, but it has never been this way.

This will not encourage a slide to disaster. It is not possible to imagine existence becoming completely negative. Existence has always had ups and downs. This process can lead to love, which is the best thing. It's not the kind of love most people associate with; it's an unconditional, openness to all aspects of life.

As we age, our fight for life's expression fades with the energy of the useless opposition. It is the blossoming of all we have without needing anything else. This flowering's ordinariness is the most difficult aspect. It all seems so ordinary, despite the grandiose illusions that youth gives off.

Each one of us is an integral part of the universe. All that we seem to be and all that is said, done, thought, or written about us are part of an inexplicable and automatic dance with the cosmos.

It doesn't matter if we are a hero or a villain. It's just a natural expression for existence. As all spiritual teachings point out, nothing can be gained or lost. The unformed, great, and unexplicable event of existence is still unformed and unexplicable.

The melodramatic youth views fade in old age and death. Instead, the vastness of our current situation propels us forward, ignoring all objections. As we age and our wilful energies diminish, it becomes clear that we are the flow of life. Even delusional people will do their part.

Fantasy is the basis of fear and the desire to control life. It is the fantasy that one can think of oneself as separate from the movement that exists, thinking that it is our responsibility to direct this movement or it will collapse.

Although there is a universal desire to recognize a higher power, the fantasy of an individual ruling the world takes precedence. This belief is often believed to be true. Life is fluid and unformed. Yet, the main focus of attention is on illusions of form or fantasies of people doing certain things in a particular world.

The indecipherable dance that is existence can be realized. It will put an end to all descriptions of me, mine, my life, and my doing. This conflicted belief is dissolved in a feeling of relief and rest.

It is false to think that spiritual life is different from worldly life. Everybody is living the best spiritual life because everything is spirit, the unformed, mysterious swirl that is all of it.

Arrogance in humans is the belief that we are superior to all other species, and that certain people are more developed than others. Either we take credit for our superiority and pass judgment on the weaknesses of others or, if one of us is the so-called inferior we take the blame for being unable to do much.

This is a fascinating view because everything in existence, including the sun, moon, clouds, seasons, weather, animals, etc., are all seen as the diverse and fascinating expressions nature. None of them is superior to the other.

It is not possible to see a bird or planet directing its development. Everything is simply an expression of the mysterious dance of existence. Everything, except one -- us. We are the ones who direct the dance.

This would imply that we exist outside of nature. It is quite strange to think that our bodies, abilities, or act ions exist somewhere other than the flow of nature. If we are not part of nature's expression, where and how do we exist?

It is impossible to know what the event of existence is. The sense of being alive disappears each night only to reappearance the next day. It's almost like a light that blinks on and off.

Our so-called "life" appears to be in flow when it's on. All of our bodies, needs, concerns, desires, urges and acts - family situations, national and international events - are temporary and disappear as if they were a part of an inanimate event.

Although there may be some hope that things will change, it doesn't guarantee that they will. The potential may exist, or it might not. Life isn't a willful act. It's a mysterious, unpredictable process that expresses itself.

It would be foolish to go to a tropical paradise to just read the brochures about the sun, sand and surf. It's easy to see how these descriptions don't capture the joy, vibrancy and excitement of an actual island paradise. We wouldn't be content to just sit and read the brochures in a hotel.

This is what most people do with their lives, focusing on the stories of our thoughts, the "brochures", of life. Spiritual awakening is the realization of the absolute emptiness in description. Instead, there is an interest in the moment itself, its unformed, mysterious, vibrant, dancing fullness.

It is incorrect to refer to existence as individuals influencing or life influencing others. Perceptual processing mistakenly sees the formless flow as distinct forms that influence each other or as a trip from one phase to the next. Even the perceptual process is misunderstood.

I am not saying to anyone "go with flow" because there is only flow. I'm not suggesting that you "be in alignment with the movement and life," because there is only one movement.

You can't be in conflict with the flow and existence.

Shades of Advaita

We are the unformed flow itself of existence; we are already and forever that.

It doesn't matter if you have any new ideas, but it is not necessary to learn anything. There is no entity called self or world outside of the imaginations of thought. There is no creation, destruction, free will, destiny, ignorance, or enlightenment. You cannot wander in the wilderness without coming to the light.

Liberation is our true nature. The unconstrained dance of all things is our true nature. While we think we are separate people, we make strenuous efforts not to be bound.

We tend to ignore the inexplicable, unformed dance of life and instead imagine bodies and minds as reality. This mistaken belief in form is what causes misery.

Reflections III

As a result, our apparent desires, needs, and concerns are referred to as an apparent thirst. It could be the desire for love, understanding and adventure, money power, knowledge, family, or other things. You may have one or more of the following.

The thirst can change from one moment to the next. It could be as simple as a need for food or entertainment. Or it could be more complex and long-term like the need to have children or understand everything. It doesn't matter what it is, at any given moment it pushes forward and sets all priorities.

Realizing that nature flows in an impersonal way doesn't make everything easy or pleasant. Nature's expressions can be ambiguous and unpleasing.

The ordinary human mind, in any moment, with all of its apparent confusions, sorrows, and wants, is already the complete and natural expression of the Divine, the Unformed, the Tao, Buddha Mind, God, Brahma, and so on. These are the various labels for the inexplicable happening that everything is.

When it's realized that every thought, word, and deed is the natural expression of existence then you're free to move without the conflict of feeling defective or incompetent. The dance of existence isn't defective or incompetent in any way.

Spiritual liberation frees you from the misery-inducing fantasy of perfecting yourself. In this moment, I am what I am; you are what you are; we're both the dance of the cosmos. Liberation isn't the act of breaking free of this. Liberation is knowing it can't be otherwise.

Just as a growing plant contains all the direction it needs to be the plant that it is, we contain all the direction we need to be the person that we are.

Everything in existence has an innate intelligence, an essential current expressing itself. Whatever you are, in any moment, is the expression of that current. There is only that current, or flow; that's what everything is.

An ocean doesn't direct its own movement; it doesn't need to struggle to express its true nature. In each moment, it's all that it can possibly be; each wave, ripple, and swirl is fine.

Fantasized notions of perfection and standards of conformity are a denial of life's flow, a denial of life's expression. Stories of individuals falling from purity to defilement are a fantasy. Nothing has fallen anywhere; everything is always the complete and natural expression of existence or, if you prefer, the expression of God.

Your fullness is whatever arises in any particular moment. This can't be classified as spiritual or worldly; it can't be classified as right or wrong: there's no way of saying what any of this actually is.

The general statement that life is about spiritual awakening, or the development of wisdom and compassion, is incorrect. That statement is merely the propaganda of groups primarily focused on spiritual matters.

Life exhibits no observable goal other than expressing itself in diverse and unique ways. For every apparent person primarily focused on wisdom and compassion, there are many who aren't. It's not that they've failed to realize a truth; they're simply a different expression of existence, an expression that's just as valid as any other.

If you're practising forgiveness, forgiving others for their behaviour, be aware that you're primarily practising judgement and blame. Before you can forgive someone you must first make them guilty of an offence.

This is a denial of life. Our urges and act ions are expressions of nature; no one can be blamed for being the particular arrangement of abilities, urges, and actions they are.

Some expressions of existence are naturally considered to be unpleasant, or even dangerous, and we will respond automatically to that unpleasantness or danger. However, just as a volcano doesn't need to be forgiven for its unpleasant, or dangerous, behaviour, neither does any person.

There is the notion that all awakened beings will behave in the same way, matching some societal fantasy of what a saint should be. In actuality, they come in all sizes, shapes, and temperaments; some are not pleasant.

They all see themselves as the inexplicable dance of existence, but this doesn't make them conform to some fantasy of perfection. It doesn't even necessarily make them sociable.

Truth, reality, God — however you want to label it — is a vital presence, a dynamic event. It's not a particular object, idea, feeling, mood, and so on. It's the inexplicable flow of existence and we've never been anything apart from that.

Existence can be summed up in one short Zen verse:

Sitting quietly,
doing nothing,
spring comes, grass
grows by itself.

The same is true of everything: the ageing of the body, the movement of thoughts and moods, urges to act ion, and actions themselves. Everything simply happens, like spring coming and grass growing.

Sitting quietly, you'll find that whatever you are, in any particular moment, presents itself automatically. Needs, interests, and concerns push themselves to the front and play out in whatever way they do.

In certain times, it's light and calm; in others, dark and stormy. In each moment, it's a totally mysterious event doing what it does.

Sitting quietly, making no effort, all is revealed: a vibrant, pulsing, formless happening, simply happening. There is no goal in this, no final point; there is only what expresses itself in this moment, and whatever it appears to be now is unavoidably on its way to some other appearance.

One of the delusions of ego is that it operates outside of the flow of cause and effect and that it's able to influence that stream by introducing something new to it. But it's never been anything separate from that flow, something that could inject anything new.

Improvements appear to occur, just as downturns do, but these are the rhythmic expressions of nature, the waves of a mighty ocean; it's not anyone's personal achievement or failure.

Anyone who appears to produce something of benefit to themselves, or to the world at large, is compelled to do so. The fascination with a particular subject, an urge to explore, an intuition, a thought, an ability, or a fortunate accident, is never anyone's personal creation.

When Einstein was complimented on his discovery of the theory of relativity, he would say it simply happened, that he didn't make it happen.

There are myriad stories of scientists investigating various subjects and, in a moment when they were relaxing or sleeping, making no effort whatsoever — not even focusing on their interest — some great discovery popped up in a thought, a vision, or a dream.

This is not a matter of "discovery"; this is simply the inexplicable dance of existence expressing itself.

We can't have up without down, joy without sorrow, confidence without anxiety, and so on. These are the natural expressions of life. If existence appears to move one way now, it will move in the apparently opposite direction at some point. This has nothing to do with anyone's efforts; this is the natural rhythm of existence.

There's nothing we can do to change this. Even if we live in the wisest way possible, existence will continue to express itself in this manner. Life is always a unique blend of apparent opposites and there's no "me" that gets to choose the mix.

The waxing and waning of emotions and states of mind are like the flowing of the seasons. We may anticipate them and prepare for them, but we can't prevent them. We don't exist as anything apart from that flow.

If I say to you there is no me, no you, no self, no world, no thinking, no personal actions, no forms of any kind, I'm not talking about some experience that's different from yours.

This is not describing some altered state; I'm pointing to the basic happening that you are right now; it's simply being acknowledged precisely.

Spiritual awakening or enlightenment doesn't add anything more to what's existing. Instead, it's the fading away of fantasies. What then remains is what has been here all along, an inexplicable dance.

When I say that's what remains, don't get the idea of some strange experience without thought. What is usually called a me, a you, a self, and a world, including thought -that still happens — but there's no longer any   obsessive belief in those false forms and labels. Instead, the absolutely inexplicable movement, or unformed flowing, that everything is becomes obvious.

Question and Answer: Part II

Q: *I want to ask you about the basic qualities that are said to arise with spiritual awakening, such as compassion, detachment, and harmony. You've touched on some of these already, but I want to take more time with them.*

I thought we could start with a consideration of compassion. Within most spiritual circles, the theme of compassion is very strong. We're urged to cultivate it and it's often coupled with wisdom as the ultimate expression of existence.

DB: Yes, people in spiritual circles often believe that wisdom and compassion are the goals of existence. They fantasize that an awakened being becomes some extraordinary fountain of love, giving endlessly to the greater good of humankind. They tend to ignore the stories of enlightened beings who, upon awakening, left society to live on their own.

Awakened beings don't gain the power to throw off their personalities; they continue to be expressions of nature. It's ironic that people have preconceived notions of what an enlightened personality is, or how that personality will behave, because each expression of nature is unique.

Some teach; some don't. Some talk; some don't. Some enjoy society; some don't. Some are pleasant personalities; some not. Some are married; some single. Some sexual; some celibate. Some live in a traditional religious environment; others do not. Some sit quietly for long periods; others don't. Some seem to make sense; others seem to be crazy. And so on.

What they have in common is the absolute certainty that everything is an unformed, inexplicable happening presenting itself.

Realizing this mysterious dance gives rise to a natural tolerance for all of life's expressions. Not only a tolerance, but the acknowledgment and appreciation that everyone is a unique expression and has to be that particular expression.

This is the compassion of awakening. It doesn't necessarily mean we like all things, or endlessly serve others, but we can appreciate that everything must be whatever it is in any particular moment.

Some awakened beings appear to serve in extraordinary ways; others appear to be nothing more than mildly good-natured; some may even appear be grouchy and intolerant. No one knows what any of this actually is and anyone who says they do is deluded.

Q: *What about harmony? How does harmony arise?*

DB: Harmony is contentment with life as it is, with all of its inevitable expressions. Seeing that everything is an expression of the cosmos, there's no longer the desire for anything more than what it offers.

Q: *How do we know what it offers?*

DB: Whatever happens is what it offers. There's never any mistake, because all of life is the impersonal expression of nature.

Q: *And seeing this is detachment?*

DB: Yes. It eventually doesn't matter what thought wants, because the various expressions of nature don't move to the wishes of thought; thought is simply one of the various expressions. Anything that appears to arise is unavoidably on its way to another expression, so why get attached to any of it?

This is not saying that with detachment there will never be desire, sorrow, confusion, anxiety, and so on. It's not saying that you won't participate in society. Life will continue to express whatever it expresses, but there's no extended concern over anything that happens. All of it is felt to be the complete and natural movement of existence. That's detachment.

Q: *What about love? In the Advaita tradition, one often hears old masters saying things like, "You are not the body; you are not the mind; there is only love."*

DB: Yes, that's the traditional expression; Robert Adams used to say it all the time. Love, in its highest philosophical sense, is an openness to all that life offers.

Everything, just as it is in any particular moment, is the complete and natural expression of existence moving to its inherent nature. Love is the simple acknowledgement of that.

Profound spiritual teachings are not prescriptions for perfecting life. They simply point to the already complete and pure expression of existence. There's the realization that everything is happening the only way it can. Realizing this brings a sense of contentment to life, with all of its apparent joys, sorrows, conflicts, and brutalities.

Again, be careful with this. It's not saying that you'll sit around doing nothing and never oppose or pursue anything; it's simply saying that whatever happens, in any apparent moment, is the unavoidable expression of existence. Nothing else is possible.

In spiritual circles we're often urged to move deep within ourselves to find a place of peace, but this is misleading. The place of our life is always the fullness of the present moment. Awakening isn't about moving to a different place; it's about a different sense of the same place.

As long as there's the fantasy that you're directing existence, life will never be enough. With the realization that everything is a movement of the cosmos, an underlying sense of peace, well-being, and openness is present in some variation, no matter what happens, because all of it is felt to be the natural dance of existence.

That peace, well-being, and openness is often called love.

Q: *How does humility arise?*

DB: What could be more humbling than to discover you're not personally responsible for anything you think, say, and do? You can no longer praise yourself for positive things; they can only be appreciated. You can no longer wallow in self-pity or recrimination for any so-called negative things; they can only be lived out.

The belief in personal doing is replaced with the simple acknowledgment of life's mysterious dance. This is not some cold, sterile, situation; it's exactly the same event that is usually perceived as people in a world. The labels and stories still arise as part of the flow, but there's no sense of understanding any of it; it simply happens, a vibrantly rich and magical parade of appearances.

Q: *When all is said and done, where does this leave us?*

DB: We continue to be whatever nature expresses in any particular moment. The ignorant assumption that it could ever be otherwise comes to an end.

Life will not express itself in a continuously calm and clear fashion. In certain periods, there can be stomach-twisting, head-pounding energies pushing and pulling in many directions, with no indication of how it will all play out.

The natural current of life is showing itself just as much in periods of intense vagueness and confusion as it is in periods of certainty and clarity.

The average so-called person isn't comfortable as the process they are. Most of us feel inadequate, or inferior, to others who appear to be more competent and happy. The most judgemental human beings are often the students of spiritual teachings. Not because they intentionally want to judge others, but because they carry the fantasy of a perfect being and hope to become that.

This hopeful fantasy doesn't allow for periods of confusion, anger, jealousy, fear, aggression, and so on. Many people view those expressions as being tainted and distorted in some way and will fall into periods of self-loathing for exhibiting this natural human behaviour.

Can you imagine a robin covering its face with its wing as it breaks down, sobbing, *"I can't believe I chirp and eat worms. Why, why, why can't I get rid of this behaviour?"* You laugh, but is it any different from a meditator sobbing, *"Why do I still get angry, jealous, fearful, and confused?"*

How many of us have prepared ourselves to act in a reasonable, calm manner when anticipating an upcoming stressful situation, but, when the moment actually arrives, we find ourselves emotionally unhinged?

This isn't our personal failure; it's the fact that our will is not ruling existence. We're a movement of nature and, no matter what the mind wishes, we have to be whatever nature expresses in any particular moment.

If there's a profound realization of this, there can be moments of absolute clarity regarding the truth of it, the feeling that there is nowhere else to get to, and nothing else to be, other than whatever presents itself in each instant. All of it is a fascinating and totally inexplicable event presenting itself.

Initially, even with deep realization, this clarity can alternate with the old illusion of being someone separate from the world, a someone desperately needing understanding and control.

At first, there will be the desire for this fluctuation to end, leaving only the feeling of clarity, but as it becomes obvious that this fluctuation is also life's natural expression, it ceases to be worrisome. At times, existence may literally feel like one great ocean moving and shifting and, at other times, that universal sense may be barely noticeable. Eventually, though, the idea that life is our doing comes to an end.

Right now, my favourite spiritual story is one of a Zen master who's dying and his students have gathered to witness his passing.

Zen masters have a reputation for uttering something profound just before they expire. There was one who, upon hearing a squirrel running across the roof tiles, sat up proclaiming, *"Just this; nothing more"*, before falling back dead. Others have uttered marvellous poems on the links between human life and nature's flow. Consequently, these particular students are waiting in great anticipation for the final moments.

The master is having trouble speaking, so he's given paper and brush to enable him to make a statement. He writes something, hands the paper back, and the students read, *"I don't want to die."*

Surprised by this, since it seems to express desire, and believing that Zen masters are beyond such human traits, the students immediately assume it must have a deeper meaning. They again give the master paper and brush, begging him to explain the real meaning of his words. Once more the old man writes something and gives the paper back. This time the students read, *"I really, really, don't want to die."*

The point is this: the master is free to be whatever he is, without apology or regret. The students, however, live in fantasies of what life should be; they're unable to acknowledge the simple facts of the moment, the simple expression of existence.

In this moment, you may love your life or you may hate it. You may be confused and frightened or clear and calm. You may be on a spiritual path or a course of crime. You may be a worldly success or a failure. You may be living to feed the poor or living only to acquire money. You may be anything a human being can appear to be and not for one moment have you stopped being the complete and pure expression of existence.

Q: *That seems like the perfect note to end on. Thank you for taking the time and trouble to do this.*

DB: I'm not doing this, and you're welcome.
Nothing ever comes to stay, to "be".
There is no "being", only endless becoming.

But there's never any real becoming.
Nothing comes to stay, to "be".

Nothing ever "is",
There is no "isness", only change, or movement.

But there's never any real change or movement. There's never any "thing" to change, to move.

There's simply the absence of form.
Movement is the ongoing absence of form.

But there's never any real absence of form.
Form has never existed. How could it possibly be absent?

Nothing is ever established or defined. There is no arriving. There is no being, no "isness", no becoming.
No thing, no change, no movement.
No presence and no absence.

Just this. Just this.
Life's struggle is
just
a lack of light, the sense of rush

and endless flight,
a ripple's vain and angst-filled fight to find its way back
to an
ever-shifting sea, when all the while nothing else exists.
There is no you; there is no me; and yet it is so nice
to dream so,
until a moment's
sanity erodes that long held fallacy, and leaves just one
great truth-filled pulse.
Mind comes before all things.
What kind of foolishness is that?
Illusion comes before a mind;
that has always been the fact.
All form is truly without form, and mind, another form along the way.
It's just a
misconception
, an ocean, now, at play.
A great ocean, whose tides and rivers appear as
things, gives birth to newborn babes,
and the river's way is written
in their new and pudgy flesh.

I think of words
to paint life's mighty sea, but they are never as splendid as the real thing. For
oceans are a vital dance,
beyond the mind's
caprice, and live a life
of liberty outside of thought's convention.
They never stop, these pains of change. Internal surging, exquisite bursting
seams of present comfort.
Moving now, receding,
then driving forth again. Ever pulsing, never arriving.
Life.
What greater law to serve than life's determined flow?
What greater will to follow
than the manifesting now?
What greater love to live
than the present sweet, sweet storm?
Life's ocean never changes: heave
and roll, in fine-spun
mist, conception.

This movement
round the unfold enfolds
twice times more than we can
imagine and left agog is truly awe,
enticing only yes. For what else can be done?

And all
the
struggles
cease.

Endnotes

This book is primarily composed of fragments from conversations with various people over many years.

Taoist Echoes and *Shades of Advaita*, were prompted by the teachings of the Taoist masters, Lao Tzu, Chuang Tzu, and Lieh Tzu, and the twentieth century Advaita master, Ramana Maharshi, as presented in the works of Timothy Freke and David Godman resp ectively. *"Echoes"* and *"Shades"* were originally much longer pieces for my own enjoyment. They're not a collection of exact quotations, but carry the essential message of the original texts.

Advaita is an ancient teaching of India; so is Buddhism. Taoism is an early teaching of China. Chan (Zen) also began in China, and is basically Buddhism mixed with Taoism.